Easy-to-Make

Beaded Jewelry

STYLISH LOOKS TO STRING, WRAP & WEAR

DESIGN ORIGINALS

an Imprint of Fox Chapel Publishing
www.d-originals.com

We would like to acknowledge the extremely talented creative team at Cousin Corporation of America for their contributions to this book. A special thanks to Kristine Regan Daniel, Jennifer Eno-Wolf, and Chloe Pemberton for their additional support.

Acquisition editor: Peg Couch
Cover and page designers: Llara Pazdan & Justin Speers
Layout designer: Wendy Reynolds
Editors: Colleen Dorsey & Katie Weeber
Technical editor: Melissa Younger
Copy editor: Laura Taylor
Photography: Mike Mihalo
Photography styling: Llara Pazdan, Kati Erney & Kate Lanphier

ISBN 978-1-4972-0310-5

© 2017 by Cousin Corporation of America and New Design Originals Corporation, *www.d-originals.com*, an imprint of Fox Chapel Publishing, 800-457-9112, 1970 Broad Street, East Petersburg, PA 17520.

Library of Congress Cataloging-in-Publication Data

Names: Daniel, Kristine Regan, author.
Title: Easy-to-make beaded jewelry / Kristine Regan Daniel.
Description: East Petersburg : Design Originals, [2017] | Includes index.
Identifiers: LCCN 2017006731 | ISBN 9781497203105 (pbk.)
Subjects: LCSH: Beaded jewelry.
Classification: LCC TT860 .D35 2017 | DDC 745.594/2--dc23
LC record available at https://lccn.loc.gov/2017006731

Printed in the United States of America
First printing

You Can DIY This!

Jewelry making should be simple, right? String a collection of beautiful beads onto a wire, attach a clasp, and you're ready to go! But when you sit down to make a project, you might feel overwhelmed by all of the techniques and vocabulary. What is the difference between a cone and a bicone, and how exactly do you use jump rings to attach the clasp? Don't be intimidated—this book is specifically designed to break it all down and keep things simple so you can unleash your creativity without fear. You'll build a foundation first, learning the basic vocabulary and techniques so you'll feel totally confident when you sit down to tackle your first project.

Diving into your first project means a trip to the craft store to gather your supplies. Shopping the jewelry aisle can be intimidating. There is always a vast array of options on display, and you don't want to arrive home to discover you missed an essential component. To keep your shopping trips straightforward and simple, each project includes a shopping list you can take to the store with you. Throw this book in your bag, or use your phone to snap a photo of the list so you are never in doubt about what you need.

Once you've made a few projects, you might get the DIY itch to make a few tweaks. And you should! That's the point of making your own jewelry, right? Instructions are provided for each project so you can reproduce the design exactly as you see it, but you should never hesitate to get creative and change it up. Each of us has a unique style, favorite color palette, and favorite outfit. If a design uses gold findings and you prefer silver, don't be afraid to make it in silver! The same goes for bead color and shape. If you see something cool in the beading aisle that you'd like to try, go for it!

This book sets you up with all of the tools you'll need to master DIY jewelry making. With a touch of your unique style and creativity, you can make these projects your own. It's time to dive in and get started!

Happy crafting!

Contents

24

Clearwater Jewelry Set

26

Boho Wire Bangles

28

Ocean Dreams Twisted Necklace

30

Switch It Up Earrings Trio

32

Vintage Floral Chain Necklace

34

Nautical Bangle Set

36

Braided Seed Bead Necklace

38

Pearls & Gems Necklace

40

Sunset Medallion Necklace

42

Swirled Shell Necklace

44

Wrapped Teardrop
Earrings

46

Crystal Pendant Necklace

48

Desert Turquoise Necklace

50

Periwinkle Necklace

52

Beaded Wrap Bracelet

54

Eco Warrior Stone
Necklace

56

Autumn Glow Necklace

58

Bronze Twirl Earrings

60

Beaded Stripes Necklace

62

Crisscross Cascade Set

Getting Started

If you are totally new to jewelry making, this is the place to start.
This section will help you build a foundation by allowing you to familiarize
yourself with the common tools and materials used in jewelry making.
You'll also find step-by-step tutorials for the techniques you'll need to assemble
the projects in this book. When you're finished, you'll be able to spot a
briolette bead when shopping at the craft store and know the best way to open
and close jump rings. Once you have a grasp of the content in this
section, you'll be ready to tackle your first jewelry project!

Tools

You don't need to spend a lot of money purchasing a vast array of tools to get started with jewelry making. A few sets of pliers and a handful of extras will allow you to make all of the projects in this book. Here are the common tools of jewelry making.

A

B

C

D

THE ESSENTIALS

Needle-nose pliers (A) come to a tapered point, making them the perfect tool to get into small areas of a jewelry design. Use this tool to hold small pieces, open and close jump rings, and manipulate wire.

Round-nose pliers (B) have rounded prongs that are used for making loops in wire, head pins, or eye pins.

Crimping pliers (C) are pliers made specifically for use with crimp tubes. The specially shaped grooves in these pliers will attach a crimp tube to beading wire in the most secure way possible.

Wire cutters (D) should always be used to cut jewelry wire—do not use scissors. Regular wire cutters that you get from the hardware store will work, but flush cutters made specifically for jewelry making are recommended.

THE EXTRAS

Memory wire cutters are heavy-duty wire cutters made specifically to cut the coils of memory wire without affecting their shape.

E-6000® glue is an extra-strong craft glue. It is perfect for securing cord ends or connecting other components.

A *jewelry hammer* is a lightweight hammer used for shaping metal. This hammer has two heads—a flat head and a round head.

A *ring mandrel* is a tapered rod used to measure the size of a ring or, in the case of jewelry making, to shape a ring to a specific size.

Beading tweezers are helpful when it comes to sorting and handling beads. Their extra-fine tip means they can pick up tiny beads more easily than your fingers can. Some tweezers come with a small, spoon-like scoop on the back end for easily collecting loose beads.

A *bead reamer* is like a mini drill that comes with an assortment of tips, which are used like drill bits. The tips can clean up the edges of a hole drilled in a bead, straighten the hole, or otherwise enlarge or re-shape the hole.

Awls are sharp, pointed tools used for making holes in leather.

TOOLS & MATERIALS

Beads

Of course beads are needed for jewelry making, but you might be surprised by the vast number of shapes and sizes that are available. What is the difference between a rondelle and a briolette? Take a look at this collection of commonly used beads to learn some important terms.

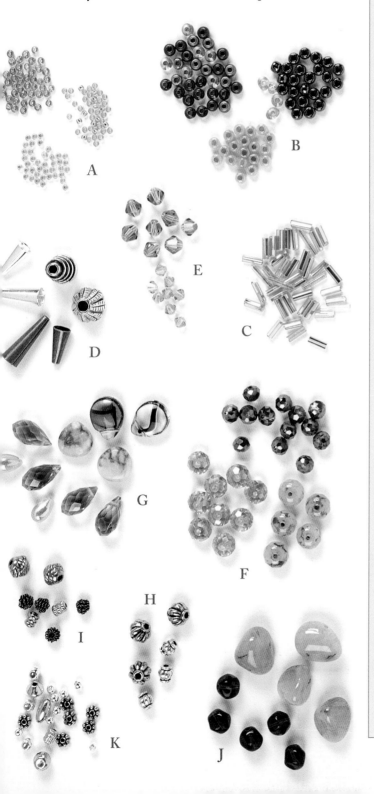

Seed beads (A) are extra-small beads, ranging in size from about 1.5mm to 3mm. Their sizes are listed as a number over zero (15/0, 12/0, etc.). The smaller the initial number, the larger the bead.

E-beads (B) are large seed beads, size 6/0, or about 4mm.

Bugle beads (C) are small, tube-shaped beads.

Cones (D) have a cone shape with a wide base at one end and a tapered point at the other. They are hollow, so they can fit over small components in a design.

Bicones (E) look like two cones that have been joined at the bottom. In profile, they have a diamond shape, with the widest point across the center and a tapered point at each end.

Rondelles (F) look like round, spherical beads that have been squashed just slightly. They look a bit like inner tubes.

Briolettes (G) have a teardrop or pear shape. They are almost always faceted (cut to have multiple faces, like a diamond) and always side-drilled, with a hole through the tapered point of the bead, rather than through the center of the bead.

Melon beads (H) actually have a pumpkin-like appearance, with raised, rounded sections running from top to bottom.

Beehive beads (I) are shaped like beehives you might see in cartoons with raised, rounded sections like rings running around the circumference of the bead.

Nuggets (J) have no specific shape. They are like pebbles you might pick up on the beach—random and unique.

Spacer beads (K) refer to small, plain, typically metallic beads. These beads serve an important function by adding space to a jewelry design without detracting from the focal beads.

Stringing Materials

Stringing materials include all of the items you can string beads onto or attach beads to. Stringing materials like cotton rope or hemp cord can also be used without beads to create jewelry using decorative knotwork. Here is a collection of common stringing materials.

B

A

D

C

E

F

Beading wire (A) is made from several thin wires twisted together and coated with a thin layer of nylon, making it very strong but also very flexible. The more strands used to make the wire, the more flexible it will be. It is used for stringing beads.

Gauge wire (B) is a single piece of metal measured by the thickness of its diameter (gauge). The smaller the gauge number, the thicker the wire is. Gauge wire has varying flexibility and can be used for stringing beads, wire wrapping, or creating fixed components in a design.

Memory wire (C) is gauge wire that has been shaped into coils. The coils can be cut or stretched, but cannot be used for wrapping or other decorative wire work.

Cord (D) generally encompasses any non-wire material used for stringing beads. It is typically made of fabric, fiber, or natural materials. Cording includes satin, leather or suede, rope, or hemp.

Monofilament (E) is an often transparent synthetic cord, similar to fishing line. It is available in different strengths based on the amount of weight it can hold (2 lb. monofilament can hold two pounds of beads).

Chain (F) is a series of metal links joined together. The links may be closed (solid pieces of metal) or open (with a slit cut through them so they can be opened and removed from the main chain). Chain is available in a variety of shapes—cable, curb, and flat-link are the types you'll encounter the most in this book. (For more about different kinds of chain, see the glossary.)

Findings

Findings are all of the components used to build a piece of jewelry. They attach, link, and hold together all of the elements in a design. Here is a collection of common jewelry findings.

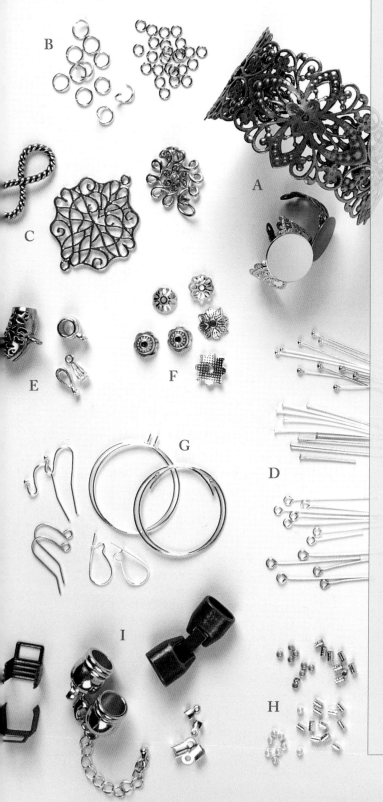

Bases (A) are unembellished blanks that you build upon to create a jewelry piece, such as a ring blank or a bangle bracelet blank.

Jump rings (B) are the most commonly used component to connect different pieces in a jewelry design. They are almost always "open" with a slit cut into the ring so it can be opened and closed. They are also available as solid rings, called closed jump rings.

Connectors (C) are bars, beads, or other components that have a loop (or loops) on each end. They are used to connect separate elements in a design.

Head pins, ball head pins, and *eye pins (D)* are short lengths of wire finished at one end with a flat head (head pin), ball (ball head pin), or loop (eye pin). Beads are strung onto the pins and the ends are formed into loops to create decorative bead drops or links.

Bails (E) are used to attach pendants to chain, cord, wire, or other stringing materials.

Bead caps (F) are bowl-shaped decorative components paired with beads. Their shape allows them to fit snugly against the bead as if they were part of it rather than a separate element.

Earring wires (G) encompass any component used to hook an earring to the ear. They come in a variety of shapes including hooks (also known as earring wires or French hooks), kidney wires, and hoops.

Crimp tubes and *crimp beads (H)* are used to finish the ends of beading wire.

Cord ends (I) are used to finish the ends of cord designs without knots. They come as caps that slide over the cord ends and are secured with glue, or crimps, which are clamped onto the cord ends.

Clasps (J, at top) are placed at the ends of a design and are used to close it. They come in numerous shapes and sizes including lobster clasps, toggle sets, or magnetic clasps.

Opening and Closing Jump Rings

Jump rings are used to connect different jewelry components to one another. Opening and closing a jump ring incorrectly can affect its shape or leave gaps that might allow jewelry components to fall off, so it's important to know how to do it properly.

Project(s) using this technique appear on pages 24, 28, 30, 32, 34, 36, 38, 40, 42, 46, 48, 50, 54, 56, 58, 60, and 62.

1 *Position the pliers.* It is best to use two needle-nose pliers for this process. Using the pliers, grasp the ring on each side of the opening.

2 *Start twisting the ring open.* To keep the ring's shape, it should be twisted open, with the ends moving back to front instead of side to side. To do this, twist one wrist toward your body and the other wrist away from your body.

3 *Finish opening the ring.* Continue twisting until the opening is wide enough to attach the desired components. String on components like chain, clasps, or bead drops.

4 *Close the ring.* Following the method in Steps 1–3, reposition the pliers and twist the ring closed. If there is a gap, gently wiggle the pliers, moving the ends of the ring backward and forward while gently pressing them together. The ends should slightly overlap and then snap together tightly so the tension of the metal will hold the ring closed.

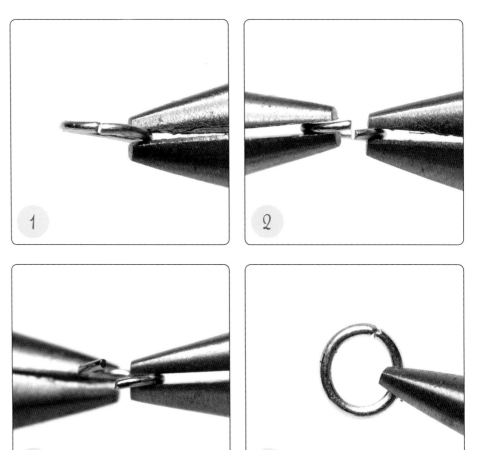

Split rings are like miniature key rings. They are made of coiled wire and do not have openings like jump rings, making them a more secure and sturdy option for heavy components. To attach items to a split ring, use a head pin or eye pin to hold the coils open.

Attaching Crimp Tubes/Beads

Crimp tubes and beads are used with beading wire and secured using crimping pliers. Once crimped, the tubes/beads stay in place on the wire, so they can be used to attach clasps or hold individual beads or groups of beads in a certain place.

Project(s) using this technique appear on pages 24, 28, 36, 38, 42, 46, 50, 54, and 56.

1. *String the clasp.* String a crimp tube and a clasp (such as one half of a toggle clasp or a single lobster clasp) onto a strand of beading wire. Bring the end of the wire back through the crimp tube, creating a ½" (1.3cm) tail. Push the crimp tube up the wire so it is close to the clasp.

2. *Make the first crimp.* Place the crimp tube in the U-shaped groove of the crimping pliers (closest to the handles). Separate the wires in the crimp tube so they are parallel and do not cross. Firmly collapse the crimp tube, forming it into a U shape with one wire in each groove.

3. *Make the second crimp.* Place the crimp tube in the oval-shaped groove of the crimping pliers (farthest from the handles). Position the crimp tube so the U shape is sideways. Squeeze the pliers so the ends of the U shape come together.

4. *Check the wire.* Once crimped, the tube will look like this. Tug on the wire to be sure it is secure. The tail of the wire can be hidden in beads strung onto the wire.

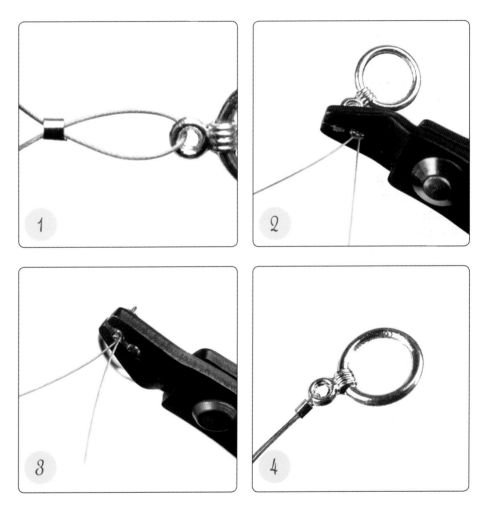

Crimp beads (below right) can be shaped using the crimp tube method described above. They are formed into smooth cylinders using the oval-shaped groove of the crimping pliers, or simply flattened using needle-nose pliers.

Cutting Chain

Jewelry projects often require lengths of chain that are shorter than what you can purchase. Use wire cutters to cut closed-link chain to the length needed. This method allows you to easily cut multiple pieces of chain to the same length without measuring each piece.

> Project(s) using this technique appear on pages 30, 32, 40, 42, 46, 48, 50, 58, and 60.

1 *Cut the first length.* Measure the length of chain needed and use wire cutters to cut it off the original chain. Remember, the cut link will fall off, so do not include this in the measurement.

2 *Cut the remaining lengths.* Thread a head pin through an end link of the cut chain, then through an end link of the original chain. Line up the chain links, and cut the next length of chain to match the first. Repeat to cut the remaining pieces needed.

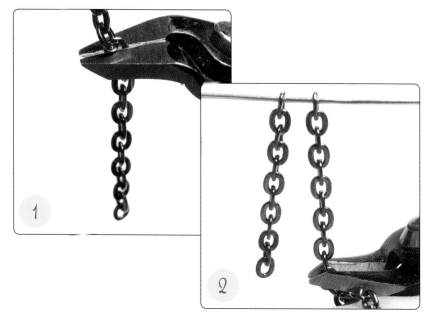

Open-Link Chain

Open chain links can be opened and closed just like jump rings (see page 12). Instead of cutting open-link chain, you can open and close the links to separate the necessary lengths of chain.

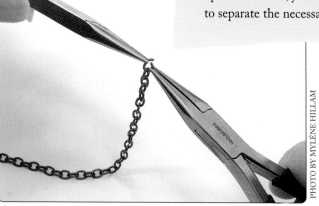

PHOTO BY MYLÈNE HILLAM

Forming a Loop

Round-nose pliers can be used to make loops in head pins, eye pins, or beading wire. Loops allow the pin or wire to be attached to other items using jump rings or other loops. Here's how to make a loop in an eye pin to create a bead link.

> Project(s) using this technique appear on pages 24, 30, 32, 34, 40, 44, 46, 48, 50, 54, 58, 60, and 62.

1 *Trim the pin.* Slide a bead (or beads) onto an eye pin. Using needle-nose pliers, bend the tail of the eye pin to form a right angle with the bead(s). Trim the tail about ¼" (0.5cm) beyond the last bead.

2 *Start forming the loop.* Grasp the end of the wire with round-nose pliers. Rotate your wrist to wrap the wire around the pliers, forming a loop. The jaws of the pliers taper, so the size of the loop can be adjusted based on its position in the pliers.

3 *Finish forming the loop.* You may need to release the pin, reposition the pliers, and rotate them again to completely close the loop.

4 *Check the finished link.* When finished, there will be a loop on each side of the bead so other components can be attached to each side.

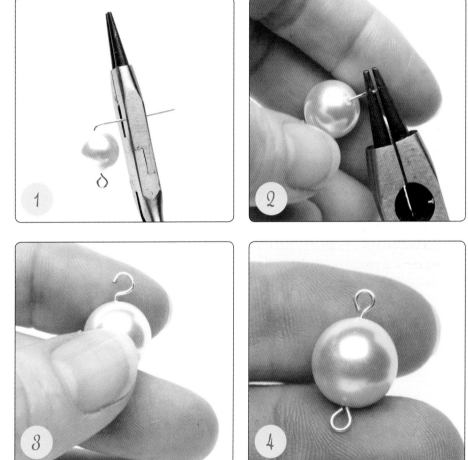

Tip: If you have trouble forming a loop at the end of a 1" (2.5cm) eye pin or head pin, you can always use a 2" (5cm) pin instead and simply trim off the excess.

Tip: You can convert a head pin to an eye pin by trimming off the flat head and forming a loop on that end instead.

Forming a Wrapped Loop

A wrapped loop is stronger than a basic loop, making it perfect for connecting heavy jewelry components. It also adds a decorative touch.

Project(s) using this technique appear on pages 24, 28, and 40.

1 **Bend the pin.** Slide a bead (or beads) onto a head pin. Grasp the head pin with round-nose pliers, resting the pliers against the top of the bead. Bend the tail of the pin to form a right angle with the bead(s).

2 **Start forming the loop.** Reposition the pliers so one prong is below the bend in the wire and one prong is above it. Wrap the tail of the head pin around the top prong, forming a loop.

3 **Finish forming the loop.** Reposition the pliers so the bottom prong is in the loop formed in Step 2. Finish forming the loop by wrapping the tail of the head pin around the bottom prong.

4 **Make the wrap.** Holding the loop with the pliers, wrap the tail of the head pin around the stem of the loop from the bottom of the loop to the top of the bead(s). Once the wrap is complete, trim away any excess from the tail of the head pin.

5 **Secure the tail.** Use needle-nose pliers or crimping pliers to tuck the trimmed tail into the wrap.

Tip: This technique works best with thin or soft metal that is pliable, like sterling.

Forming a Loop for Briolette Beads

Briolettes and other side-drilled beads require a slightly different technique for creating a loop at the top of the bead. Adding a loop gives these types of beads the appearance of a pendant or bead drop.

Project(s) using this technique appear on page 38.

1 *Make the stem.* Grasp an eye pin directly under the loop with round-nose pliers. Partially bend the tail of the pin to the side at about a 45-degree angle, below the prong of the pliers, to form a short stem under the loop.

2 *Position the pin.* With the bead flat on a surface, set the loop and stem directly above the top of the bead with the bent tail off to one side of the bead. Use the pliers to slightly mark the spot on the tail of the pin where the pin will need to bend to go into the bead hole.

3 *Make the first bend.* Thread the tail of the pin through the bead up to the spot marked in Step 2. Then bend the wire flush up against the bead to reposition the loop and stem at the top of the bead. Press the pin against the bead to shape it to the curve of the bead, using round-nose pliers to help shape it as needed.

4 *Make the second bend.* Bend the other end of the pin flush up against the other side of the bead to mirror your first bend, smoothing the pin against the side of the bead.

5 *Make the wrap.* Wrap the tail of the pin around the stem from the top of the bead to the bottom of the loop. Trim away any excess from the tail of the pin, and use needle-nose pliers or crimping pliers to tuck the tail into the wrap.

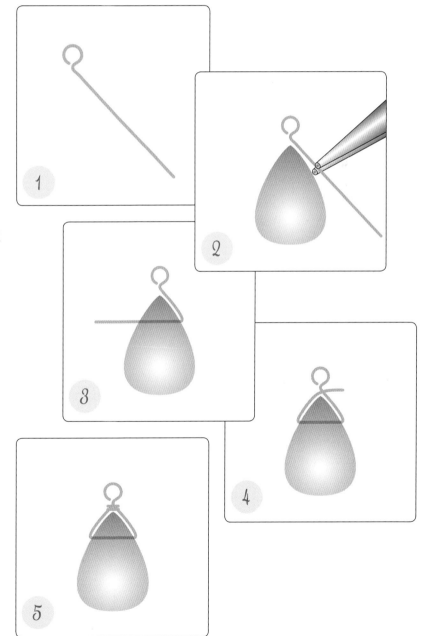

Wrapping Beads with Wire

A wire wrap is a beautiful effect to add to a bead. The technique works best on teardrop or pear-shaped beads and can be used to create embellished bead drops, pendants, or earrings.

Project(s) using this technique appear on page 44.

1. *String the bead.* String a bead onto a length of wire. Center the bead along the wire, then bend the wire up at each side of the bead. Smooth the ends of the wire up along the sides of the bead so they meet at the top.

2. *Make the loop.* Use round-nose pliers to form a loop at the top of the bead. Refer to Steps 1–3 for Forming a Wrapped Loop on page 16.

3. *Form the wrap.* Holding the loop with the pliers, wrap the tail of the wire around the stem of the loop and around the top of the bead.

4. *Trim and finish.* Continue the wrap to the desired position on the bead. Once the wrap is complete, trim away any excess wire and use needle-nose pliers to tuck the tail into the wrap.

1

2

3

4

Overhand Knot

Overhand knots can be used to start or finish a design, to hold components in place in a design, or to function as decorative elements.

Project(s) using this technique appear on page 52.

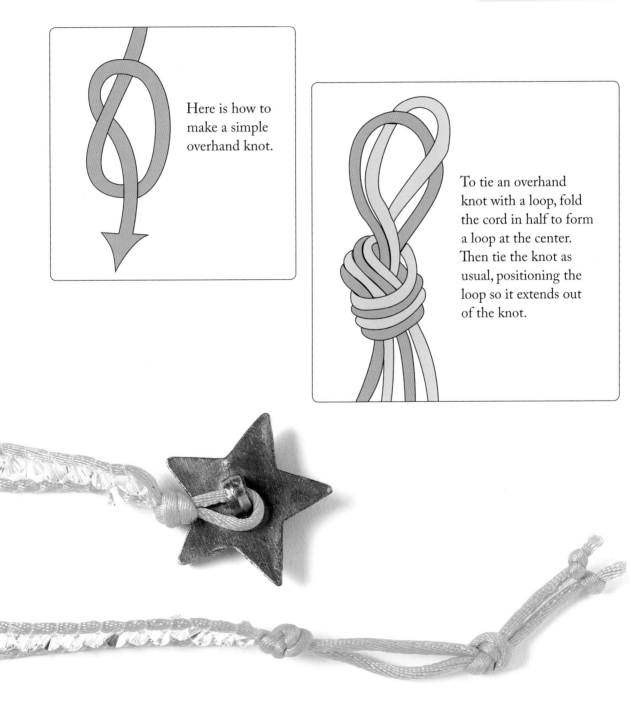

Here is how to make a simple overhand knot.

To tie an overhand knot with a loop, fold the cord in half to form a loop at the center. Then tie the knot as usual, positioning the loop so it extends out of the knot.

Braiding

Braiding is a simple technique that can be used in a variety of ways for jewelry making. Braiding pairs wonderfully with cord, rope, and ribbon and gives a unique twist to a design with beaded strands and chain.

Project(s) using this technique appear on pages 28 and 36.

1 **Start the pattern.** Place 3 cords side by side. Bring the left cord over the center cord. Then, bring the right cord over the new center cord.

2 **Repeat the pattern.** Repeat the pattern from Step 1, bringing the left cord over the center cord then the right cord over the center cord until the braid reaches the desired length.

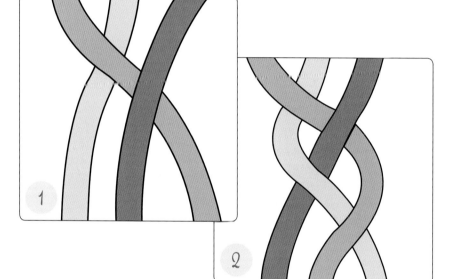

Braiding Tips

• Braid a variety of materials together, like cord, ribbon, and chain, to create interest and texture.
• Braiding beaded strands together is a great way to add movement to a simple beaded bracelet or necklace.
• Braiding can be done with more than 3 strands. Divide a large number of strands into 3 groups to create a thick braid. For example, divide 12 beaded strands into 3 groups of 4.

Surgeon's Knot

This knot is perfect for attaching one cord to another cord in such a way that the attached cord won't move or slide. For example, you can attach thin monofilament to slippery satin cord.

Project(s) using this technique appear on page 52.

1 **Make the first loop.** Lay the main cord to which you are tying the monofilament flat. Align the monofilament with the main cord so that both cords run parallel together, with one end of the monofilament about 2" (5cm) past where you actually want the knot to be on the main cord. Make a loop with the cords, laying the cords over top of themselves, then pass the cords under and through the loop.

2 **Start the second loop.** Bring the cords up over the top of the loop.

3 **Finish the second loop.** Pass the cords under and through the loop again, as you did in Step 1.

4 **Tighten the knot.** Tighten the knot by pulling the left loose cord end (the monofilament) to the left and down, and the right loose cord end (the main cord) to the right and up. Trim the excess cord as needed.

Step-by-Step Projects

Now that you know the lingo and understand the basic techniques, it's time to put what you've learned into practice and make some projects. Remember to use the shopping lists to help navigate the jewelry section at the store. And don't be afraid to choose beads and colors that suit your personal taste to make a project your own!

Level:
♦ ● ●

Time:
♦ ♦ ●

The "Level" for each project indicates whether it is Beginner, Intermediate, or Advanced.

The "Time" for each project indicates how long each project will take, not including glue drying time. One diamond means less than an hour; two diamonds means between one and two hours; and three diamonds means more than two hours.

Clearwater Jewelry Set

This set gives off a casual, coastal vibe that will pair beautifully with a sundress and a white pair of sunglasses. Wear it with gold bangles to highlight the gold in the necklace and earrings.

NECKLACE

1 *Start the necklace.* Thread a head pin through the hole in the gemstone slice and form a wrapped loop. Use a 4mm jump ring to connect the pendant to the bottom of the bail. Cut a 25" (64cm) length of beading wire. Use a crimp tube to connect a 4mm jump ring to one end of the beading wire.

2 *Start beading.* String on a 10mm turquoise round bead and a melon bead. Repeat this pattern five more times. String on a 22mm white gemstone nugget, melon bead, 6mm aqua glass round bead, melon bead, 20mm white gemstone nugget, melon bead, opal glass oval bead, melon bead, 18mm white gemstone nugget, melon bead, medium aqua flat round bead, melon bead, 14mm white gemstone nugget, melon bead, aqua glass bicone, melon bead, 10mm white gemstone nugget, and melon bead.

3 *Add the pendant.* String the bail from Step 1 onto the necklace; it should cover up the last melon bead but not the last white gemstone nugget.

4 *Continue beading.* Continue by stringing on a 10mm white gemstone nugget, melon bead, medium aqua flat square bead, melon bead, 14mm white gemstone nugget, melon bead, opal glass bicone, melon bead, 18mm white gemstone nugget, melon bead, medium aqua flat round bead, melon bead, 20mm white gemstone nugget, melon bead, aqua glass bicone, melon bead, and a 22mm white gemstone nugget. String on a melon bead and a 10mm turquoise round bead. Repeat this pattern five more times. Use a crimp tube to connect the end of the beading wire to a 4mm jump ring.

5 *Add the clasp.* Use 6mm jump rings to connect the 4mm jump rings on each end of the necklace to each half of the toggle clasp.

SHOPPING LIST

- 1 - 45 x 25mm gemstone slice pendant (blue)
- 2 - 22mm gemstone nugget beads (white)
- 2 - 20mm gemstone nugget beads (white)
- 2 - 18mm gemstone nugget beads (white)
- 2 - 14mm gemstone nugget beads (white)
- 2 - 10mm gemstone nugget beads (white)
- 12 - 10mm dyed round beads (turquoise)
- 1   8mm glass flat square bead (medium aqua)
- 1 - 6mm glass round bead (medium aqua)
- 1 - 10 x 6mm glass oval bead (opal)
- 2 - 10mm glass flat round beads (medium aqua)
- 2 - 8 x 8mm glass bicone beads (aqua)
- 1 - 8 x 8mm glass bicone bead (opal)
- 37 - 2 x 3mm melon beads (gold)
- 2 - 18 x 15mm glass nuggets (light aqua)
- 2 - 16 x 7mm dyed oval beads (turquoise)
- 25" (64cm) - Beading wire (gold)
- 1 - 10mm bail (gold)
- 2 - Crimp tubes (gold)
- 2 - 2" (5cm) eye pins (gold)
- 3 - 2" (5cm) head pins (gold)
- 7 - 4mm jump rings (gold)
- 2 - 6mm jump rings (gold)
- 2 - Earring wires (gold)
- 1 - 8mm toggle clasp set (gold)

TOOLS

- Needle-nose pliers
- Round-nose pliers
- Crimping pliers
- Wire cutters

TECHNIQUES

- Opening and Closing Jump Rings
- Attaching Crimp Tubes/Beads
- Forming a Loop
- Forming a Wrapped Loop

EARRINGS

1. *Create the bead link and drop.* Slide a melon bead, an 18 x 15mm aqua glass nugget, and a melon bead onto an eye pin and form a loop to make a bead link. Slide a melon bead, a 16 x 7mm turquoise oval, and a melon bead onto a head pin and form a loop to make a bead drop.

2. *Create the earring.* Use a 4mm jump ring to connect one side of the bead link to an earring wire. Use a 4mm jump ring to connect the other side of the bead link to the bead drop.

3. *Make the other earring.* Repeat Steps 1–2 for the matching earring.

Boho Wire Bangles

It's easy to dress these bracelets up or pair them with a more casual outfit. Try them with your favorite t-shirt and jeans combo or a classic work outfit. If silver is your preferred color for jewelry, substitute silver wire for the gold and have fun playing with different options for the focal beads.

1 **Create the coils.** Cut a 16" (41cm) length of 16-gauge wire. Coil the wire into a bangle shape. You should end up with the wire coiled twice with about 2" (5cm) of excess wire overlapping the coils. Wrap the excess wire ends around the coiled wires to secure the bangle shape.

2 **Cut the wrapping wire.** Cut three 36" (92cm) lengths of 24-gauge wire.

3 **Start the first wrap.** Wrap the last 2" (5cm) of a length of 36" (92cm) wire around the coiled 16-gauge wire to cover where the excess 16-gauge wire was wrapped.

4 **Add the bead.** String a bead onto the length of 24-gauge wire you are working with.

5 **Wrap the bead.** On the other side of the bead, wrap about 3" (7.5cm) of wire around the 16-gauge coils to hold the bead down against the bangle. Then wrap the wire under and around the base of the bead, parallel to the bangle, over and over again, until you have only a tail of wire measuring about 2–3" (5–7.5cm) left.

6 **Finish wrapping the bead.** Wrap the last 2–3" (5–7.5cm) of 24-gauge wire around the coiled 16-gauge wires so the wrapping looks even on each side of the bead. Trim any excess wire.

7 **Add two more beads.** About 1½" (3.8cm) beyond the last bead, repeat Steps 3–5 two more times so that you end up with three evenly spaced beads.

8 **Make the other bracelets.** Repeat Steps 1–7 for the matching bracelets.

SHOPPING LIST

- 6 - 6 x 25mm acrylic oval beads (ivory)
- 3 - 29mm gold/acrylic 2-hole beads (animal print)
- 27' (830cm) - 24-gauge wire (gold)
- 48" (125cm) - 16-gauge wire (gold)

TOOLS

- Needle-nose pliers
- Wire cutters

Ocean Dreams Twisted Necklace

Level:
◆ ● ●

Time:
◆ ◆ ●

With casual elements like suede and cord and elegant components like pearls and gems, this necklace is a perfect everyday go-to. The neutral grays and greens will look great against a white shirt. Complete the look with a pair of pearl or rhinestone stud earrings.

1 *Braid the cord.* Cut three 60" (153cm) lengths of iridescent cord. Braid them together to a length of 19" (49cm). Cut 2 short lengths of extra cord and tie them tightly around the very ends of the braid to hold the braid together. Trim off excess cords.

2 *Complete the cords.* Lay the iridescent braided cord and 19" (49cm) green suede cord together, side by side. String the 3 gunmetal/rhinestone beads onto the middle of the cord set. Attach a separate 4mm jump ring to the loops on each silver cord end. Glue each end of the cord set into the silver cord ends. Allow to dry.

3 *Bead the first wire.* Cut a 26" (66cm) length of 24-gauge wire. Form a wrapped loop at one end of the wire. String 23 blue/green pearls onto the wire, thread the wire through the 3 gunmetal/rhinestone beads, and string on 23 more blue/green pearls. Form another wrapped loop at the end of the wire. Trim off excess wire. Attach a separate 4mm jump ring to the loop at each end.

4 *Bead the second wire.* Cut a 26" (66cm) length of beading wire. Use a crimp tube to close one end of the beading wire, then attach it to a 4mm jump ring. String 41 gray pearls onto the wire, thread the wire through the 3 gunmetal/rhinestone beads, and string on 41 more gray pearls. Use a crimp tube to attach the end of the beading wire to another 4mm jump ring.

5 *Twist the strands.* Loosely twist all the strands together on each side of the center of the necklace.

6 *Finish the necklace.* Connect the 4mm jump rings on all 3 strands of each end of the necklace to a single 6mm jump ring on each side. Connect a lobster clasp to one 6mm jump ring, and use a 4mm jump ring to connect the extender chain to the other 6mm jump ring.

SHOPPING LIST

- 3 - 12 x 3mm large-hole beads (gunmetal/rhinestone)
- 46 - 10mm glass round beads (light blue/green pearl)
- 82 - 6mm glass round beads (gray pearl)
- 19" (49cm) - 10mm suede and chain braided cord (green/silver)
- 16' (490cm) - 1mm iridescent cord (light blue)
- 26" (66cm) - Beading wire (silver)
- 26" (66cm) - 24-gauge wire (silver)
- 2 - 7 x 4mm cord ends (silver)
- 2 - Crimp tubes (silver)
- 1 - 3" (7.5cm) extender chain (silver)
- 7 - 4mm jump rings (silver)
- 2 - 6mm jump rings (silver)
- 1 - Lobster clasp (silver)

TOOLS

- Needle-nose pliers
- Round-nose pliers
- Crimping pliers
- Wire cutters
- Scissors
- Tape
- Craft glue

TECHNIQUES

- Opening and Closing Jump Rings
- Attaching Crimp Tubes/Beads
- Forming a Wrapped Loop
- Braiding

Switch It Up Earrings Trio

What could be better than three earrings in one? Choose your look, and swap out the dangles of these earrings for the perfect fit. From simple drop earrings to multi-strand earrings with lots of movement, this set has you covered!

Before You Begin: Connect the loop of an earring wire to the bar half of a toggle clasp. Repeat with another earring wire and bar half of a toggle clasp. These pieces will be used as the "earring base" for each set of interchangeable earrings.

CLUSTER EARRINGS

1 *Create the bead drops.* Slide a metallic brown bead onto a head pin and form a loop. Repeat to make a total of 5 brown bead drops. Slide a purple splatter bead onto a head pin and form a loop. Repeat to make a total of 5 purple bead drops. Slide a green crackle bead onto a head pin and form a loop. Repeat to make a total of 5 green bead drops.

2 *Prepare the chain.* Cut the following lengths of chain: one 1½" (3.8cm), one 1¼" (3.2cm), and one 1" (2.6cm). Use a 4mm jump ring to connect one end of each length of chain to the circle half of a toggle clasp.

3 *Create the bead clusters.* Use one 6mm jump ring to connect the 5 purple bead drops to the other end of the 1½" (3.8cm) length of chain, the 5 brown bead drops to the other end of the 1¼" (3.2cm) length of chain, and the 5 green bead drops to the other end of the 1" (2.6cm) length of chain.

4 *Make the other earring.* Repeat Steps 1–3 for the matching earring.

TRIPLE CHAIN BEAD DROP EARRINGS

1 *Create the bead drop.* Slide a purple splatter bead, metallic brown bead, and green bead onto a head pin and form a loop to make a bead drop.

2 *Prepare the chain.* Cut three 1" (2.5cm) lengths of chain. Use a 4mm jump ring to connect one end of each length of chain to the circle half of a toggle clasp.

3 *Add the bead drops.* Use another 4mm jump ring to connect the other end of each length of chain to the loop of the bead drop.

4 *Make the other earring.* Repeat Steps 1–3 for the matching earring.

SHOPPING LIST

- 14 - 6mm round beads (metallic brown)
- 14 - 6mm round beads (purple splatter)
- 14 - 6mm round beads (green crackle)
- 16" (41cm) - 2.3mm cable chain (antique gold)
- 34 - 1" (2.5cm) head pins (antique gold)
- 8 - 4mm jump rings (antique gold)
- 6 - 6mm jump rings (antique gold)
- 2 - Earring wires (antique gold)
- 6 - 10mm toggle clasp sets (antique gold)

TOOLS

- Needle-nose pliers
- Round-nose pliers
- Wire cutters

TECHNIQUES

- Opening and Closing Jump Rings
- Cutting Chain
- Forming a Loop

SIMPLE BEAD DROP EARRINGS

1. *Create the bead drop.* Slide a purple splatter bead, metallic brown bead, and green bead onto a head pin and form a loop to make a bead drop.

2. *Add the clasp.* Use a 4mm jump ring to connect the loop of the bead drop to the circle half of a toggle clasp.

3. *Make the other earring.* Repeat Steps 1–2 for the matching earring.

Vintage Floral Chain Necklace

With its floral elements and vintage charm, this necklace is the perfect piece to pair with a springy dress or your favorite t-shirt and jeans. For more vintage flair, use a silk floral scarf as a headband or purse accent.

1 *Make the bead links.* Slide a floral cluster bead onto an eye pin and form a loop. Repeat to make a total of 2 floral cluster bead links.

2 *Add the connector.* Connect the loop on one side of each floral cluster bead link to the loops on each side of the bubble bird print connector.

3 *Cut the small chains.* Cut a 5½" (14cm) and a 6½" (16.5cm) length of cable chain.

4 *Add the small chains.* Use a single 4mm jump ring to connect one end of both cable chains to the outside loop of one of the floral cluster bead links from Step 2. Use another 4mm jump ring to connect the other end of both cable chains to the outside loop of the other floral cluster bead link so that the longer chain drapes below the shorter one.

5 *Add the necklace chains.* Cut two 8" (21cm) lengths of double-link curb chain. Connect one end of each length to the top of each 4mm jump ring from Step 4.

6 *Add the clasp.* Use 6mm jump rings to connect the other end of one 8" (21cm) double-link curb chain to a lobster clasp and the other 8" (21cm) chain to the extender chain.

SHOPPING LIST

- 1 - 42mm bubble bird print connector (gold/pink/blue)
- 2 - 20mm clay side-drilled floral cluster beads (green/pink/blue)
- 16" (42cm) - 7mm double-link curb chain (antique gold)
- 12" (31cm) - 2 x 3mm cable chain (antique gold)
- 1 - 3" (7.5cm) - extender chain (antique gold)
- 2 - 2" (5cm) eye pins (antique gold)
- 2 - 4mm jump rings (antique gold)
- 2 - 6mm jump rings (antique gold)
- 1 - Lobster clasp (antique gold)

TOOLS

- Needle-nose pliers
- Round-nose pliers
- Wire cutters

TECHNIQUES

- Opening and Closing Jump Rings
- Cutting Chain
- Forming a Loop

Nautical Bangle Set

This bangle set has an all-out nautical style that's perfect for any summer vacation. Show these off on the boardwalk or during happy hour with friends. Substitute beads in your favorite coastal colors or your favorite ocean-inspired charms.

Before You Begin: Cut the memory wire into three equal lengths.

LIVE YOUR DREAM BRACELET

1 *Bead the wire.* Attach a 4mm jump ring to the compass charm. Take one length of memory wire and string on all of the blue faceted round beads and then the compass charm. During the next two steps, keep the beads and charm centered on the wire.

2 *Form the closure.* Form a loop at one end of the wire. Pass the other end of the wire through this loop. Form a loop at the other end of the wire, making sure it goes around the wire next to it.

3 *Add the final charm.* Use a 4mm jump ring to connect the "Live Your Dream" charm to one of the wires in the section of the bracelet where the wires crisscross.

SAILING BRACELET

1 *Bead the wire.* Take one length of memory wire and string on all of the oval beads. During the next two steps, keep the beads centered on the wire.

2 *Form the closure.* Repeat Step 2 from the Live Your Dream Bracelet above.

3 *Add the charms.* Connect the jump ring of the blue tassel to both of the wires in the section of the bracelet where the wires cross. Use 4mm jump rings to connect the sailboat and boat wheel charms to one of the wires in the section of the bracelet where the wires crisscross.

CLAMSHELL BRACELET

1 *Bead the wire.* Take one length of memory wire and string on all of the white pearl rondelles and the clamshell slide bead. During the next two steps, keep the beads centered on the wire.

2 *Form the closure.* Form a loop at the end of the wire next to the clamshell slide bead. Pass the other end of the wire through this loop and the slide bead. Form a loop at the other end of the wire, making sure it goes around the wire next to it.

3 *Add the tassel.* Connect the jump ring of the teal tassel to both of the wires in the section of the bracelet where the wires crisscross.

SHOPPING LIST

- 35 - 8mm rondelle beads (white pearl)
- 17 - 10mm faceted round beads (blue)
- 14 - 11 x 8mm oval beads (turquoise)
- 1 - Compass charm (silver)
- 1 - "Live Your Dream" charm (silver)
- 1 - Sailboat charm (silver)
- 1 - Boat wheel charm (silver)
- 1 - Clamshell slide bead (silver)
- 1 - Tassel with jump ring (blue)
- 1 - Tassel with jump ring (teal)
- 5+ - Coils memory wire, 3" (7.5cm) diameter (silver)
- 4 - 4mm jump rings (silver)

TOOLS

- Needle-nose pliers
- Round-nose pliers
- Wire cutters
- Memory wire cutters

TECHNIQUES

- Opening and Closing Jump Rings
- Forming a Loop

Braided Seed Bead Necklace

With its earthy, metallic beads, this necklace easily makes the transition from day to evening. This design is easy to customize to fit your style. Just substitute the gold and brown beads for ones in your favorite colors. Try bright neons for a fun pop of color or black and silver for a neutral classic.

1 **Prepare the wires.** Cut nine 36" (92cm) lengths of beading wire. Take 3 wires and use crimp tubes to attach one end of each wire to a single jump ring. Repeat with the remaining wires so that you have 3 jump rings with 3 wires attached to each.

2 **Connect the jump rings.** Gather the 3 jump rings from Step 1 onto a single new jump ring so that all 9 wires are gathered.

3 **String one section.** String 31" (79cm) of E-beads (all the same color) onto 1 of the beading wires. Use crimp tubes to connect the end of the beaded strand to a new jump ring. Repeat to string the same color of beads on the remaining 2 beading wires that are attached to the same jump ring as the first wire, ending each strand on the same new jump ring.

4 **String the remaining two sections.** Repeat Step 3 twice more with the remaining beading wires and 2 additional bead colors.

5 **Braid.** Braid the 3 sets of beaded strands together.

6 **Finish.** Secure the end of the braid by gathering the 3 jump rings onto a single new jump ring (as in Step 2) and adding the lobster clasp to the final jump ring.

SHOPPING LIST

- 650+ - 6/0 E-beads (topaz)
- 650+ - 6/0 E-beads (metallic brown mix)
- 650+ - 6/0 E-beads (opaque brown)
- 27' (830cm) - Beading wire (gold)
- 18 - Crimp tubes (gold)
- 8 - 6mm jump rings (gold)
- 1 - Lobster clasp (gold)

TOOLS

- Needle-nose pliers
- Crimping pliers
- Wire cutters

TECHNIQUES

- Opening and Closing Jump Rings
- Attaching Crimp Tubes/Beads
- Braiding

Pearls & Gems Necklace

A blazer or jacket will highlight the focal section of this necklace beautifully. Add a pearl bracelet or earrings to enhance the look. The greens and blues of this design will also pair nicely with silver findings, if that is your preferred color for the chain and wire.

Level:
◈ ◈ ●

Time:
◈ ◈ ●

1 *Prepare the chains.* Cut the chain into two 6½" (16.5cm) lengths. Use a 4mm jump ring to connect a lobster clasp to one end of one length of chain; connect a 6mm jump ring to one end of the other length of chain. Connect a separate 4mm jump ring to the other end of each chain, and then connect a separate closed 4mm jump ring to each open 4mm jump ring.

2 *Make the spike drops.* Thread an eye pin through the hole in a turquoise spike and form a wrapped briolette loop. Repeat to make a total of 12 spike drops.

3 *Make the druzy drops.* Thread an eye pin through the hole in a druzy pendant and form a wrapped briolette loop. Repeat to make a total of 5 druzy drops.

4 *Attach the wire.* Use a crimp tube to connect one end of the 10" (26cm) length of beading wire to the closed 4mm jump ring on the end of one length of chain from Step 1.

5 *Start stringing the wire.* String the following onto the beading wire: 6mm white pearl, spike drop, 4mm white pearl, spike drop, 6mm white pearl, druzy drop, 6mm white pearl, spike drop, 4mm white pearl, spike drop, 6mm white pearl, druzy drop, 6mm white pearl, spike drop, 4mm white pearl, spike drop, and a 6m white pearl.

6 *Finish stringing the wire.* String on a druzy drop, then repeat Step 5 in reverse.

7 *Finish the necklace.* Use a crimp tube to connect the end of the bead strand to the closed 4mm jump ring on the end of the other length of chain from Step 1.

SHOPPING LIST

- 5 - 28 x 20mm side-drilled druzy pendants (green onyx/turquoise)
- 12 - 28 x 2.5mm spike drops (turquoise)
- 12 - 6mm glass round beads (white pearl)
- 6 - 4mm glass round beads (white pearl)
- 13" (33cm) - 1.8mm cable chain with 3mm round beads (gold)
- 10" (26cm) - Beading wire (gold)
- 2 - Crimp tubes (gold)
- 17 - 2" (5cm) eye pins (gold)
- 3 - 4mm jump rings (gold)
- 2 - 4mm closed jump rings (gold)
- 1 - 6mm jump ring (gold)
- 1 - Lobster clasp (gold)

TOOLS

- Needle-nose pliers
- Round-nose pliers
- Crimping pliers
- Wire cutters

TECHNIQUES

- Opening and Closing Jump Rings
- Attaching Crimp Tubes/Beads
- Forming a Loop for Briolette Beads

Sunset Medallion Necklace

This long pendant necklace is a fun summertime piece. The neutral gemstone and light chain give it a casual look, while the gold filigree and rhinestone beads add a bit of sparkle and shine. If you prefer cool colors, use silver chain and beads and a green or blue gemstone.

1   *Create coin bead links.* Slide a gold coin onto an eye pin and form a loop. Repeat to make a total of 4 coin bead links.

2   *Create melon bead links.* Slide a gold melon onto an eye pin and form a loop. Repeat to make a total of 2 melon bead links.

3   *Cut chain.* Cut two 5½" (14cm) and six 2" (5cm) lengths of chain.

4   *Create the necklace halves.* Connect the following, in order: 5½" (14cm) chain, coin bead link, 2" (5cm) chain, melon bead link, 2" (5cm) chain, coin bead link, and 2" (5cm) chain. Repeat one more time to make a total of 2 chain/bead link strands.

5   *Add the clasp.* Connect one end of the extender chain to a 6mm jump ring. Use a 4mm jump ring to connect one 5½" (14cm) chain from Step 4 to the 6mm jump ring. Use a 4mm jump ring to connect the end of the other 5½" (14cm) chain from Step 4 to a lobster clasp.

6   *Connect the necklace halves.* Cut (or separate) a single link of chain from the extra chain. Use this link to join together the ends of the 2" (5cm) chains of each strand from Step 4.

7   *Create bead drops.* Slide a rhinestone round and a gold coin onto a head pin and form a loop. Repeat this step to make a total of 4 bead drops.

8   *Finish the extender.* Connect 1 bead drop from Step 7 to the end of the extender chain from Step 5.

9   *Cut more chain.* Cut one ¾" (2cm) and two ⅜" (1cm) lengths of chain.

SHOPPING LIST

- 1 - 48 x 30mm natural agate gemstone pendant
- 8 - 10mm flat coin beads (gold)
- 2 - 9mm melon beads (gold)
- 4 - 6mm rhinestone round beads (gold/clear)
- 1 - 46 x 30mm filigree connector (gold)
- 30" (77cm) - 2 x 3mm cable chain (gold)
- 1 - 3" (7.5cm) extender chain (gold)
- 4 - 2" (5cm) head pins (gold)
- 7 - 1" (2.5cm) eye pins (gold)
- 8 - 4mm jump rings (gold)
- 1 - 6mm jump ring (gold)
- 1 - Lobster clasp (gold)

TOOLS

- Needle-nose pliers
- Round-nose pliers
- Wire cutters

TECHNIQUES

- Opening and Closing Jump Rings
- Cutting Chain
- Forming a Loop
- Forming a Wrapped Loop

10 *Start the pendant.* Use 4mm jump rings to connect a bead drop from Step 7 to one end of each length of chain from Step 9. With the longer chain in the middle, use three 4mm jump rings to connect the other end of each chain to a loop on one end of a gold filigree connector.

11 *Finish the pendant.* Open the "eye" of an eye pin and connect it to the single chain link added in Step 6. Thread the stem of the eye pin, back to front, through the hole of the agate pendant, then through the loop on the other end of the filigree connector, so that the filigree connector hangs flat in front of the agate pendant. Bring the stem of the eye pin back up and form a wrapped loop just below the eye in the eye pin. Trim excess wire.

Level:
💎 💎 ○

Time:
💎 💎 ○

Swirled Shell Necklace

This multi-strand necklace is a cleverly understated statement piece. It will show off your style without being over the top, making it perfect for work or casual wear. The shell beads give it a light, summery feel. Try it with cropped ankle pants and a pair of wedges.

1 *Cut the wire.* Cut the following lengths of beading wire: 7" (18cm), 9" (23cm), and 11" (28cm). Using crimp tubes, attach each wire to its own 4mm jump ring on one end.

2 *String the first wire.* String the following pattern onto the 7" (18cm) wire: a bicone, a white oval, a bicone, a purple hexagon, a bicone, a white oval, a bicone, a purple hexagon, a bicone, a white oval, and a bicone.

3 *String the second wire.* String the following pattern onto the 9" (23cm) wire: a bicone, a white oval, a bicone, a purple hexagon, a bicone, a white oval, a bicone, a purple hexagon, a bicone, a white oval, a bicone, a purple hexagon, a bicone, a white oval, and a bicone.

4 *String the third wire.* String the following pattern onto the 11" (28cm) wire: a bicone, a white oval, a bicone, a purple hexagon, a bicone, a white oval, a bicone, a purple hexagon, a bicone, a white oval, a bicone, a purple hexagon, a bicone, a white oval, a bicone, a purple hexagon, a bicone, a white oval, and a bicone.

5 *Finish each wire.* Using crimp tubes, attach each wire to its own 4mm jump ring to close off the string of beads. Trim the excess wire.

6 *Cut the chains.* Cut twelve 8" (20cm) lengths of chain. Attach 2 chains to each 4mm jump ring.

7 *Finish one side.* Gather the other ends of the 6 chains from one side of the necklace onto a 6mm jump ring. Attach one half of a toggle clasp to the 6mm jump ring.

8 *Finish the other side.* Use another 6mm jump ring to repeat Step 7, attaching the other ends of the 6 other chains to the other half of the toggle clasp.

SHOPPING LIST

- 9 - 14mm dyed hexagon shell beads (purple/black)
- 12 - 18 x 12mm dyed oval shell beads (white/black)
- 24 - 4mm glass bicone beads (copper)
- 28" (71cm) - Beading wire (gold)
- 9' (275cm) - 2 x 3mm curb chain (copper)
- 6 - Small crimp tubes (copper)
- 6 - 4mm jump rings (copper)
- 2 - 6mm jump rings (copper)
- 1 - Small toggle clasp set (copper)

TOOLS

- Needle-nose pliers
- Crimping pliers
- Wire cutters

TECHNIQUES

- Opening and Closing Jump Rings
- Attaching Crimp Tubes/Beads
- Cutting Chain

Wrapped Teardrop Earrings

The teardrop shape of these earrings gives them a timeless, classic look while the wire wrap adds a modern twist. These will pair beautifully with a simple, streamlined updo and a little black dress.

1 *Form the frame.* Cut a 6" (15.5cm) length of 16-gauge wire. Form the wire around a teardrop bead, making a close-fitting frame for the bead.

2 *Form the loop.* Trim one side of the wire ¼" (0.7cm) past where the two wires meet. Trim the other end snug against the first wire. Use round-nose pliers to form a closed loop with the ¼" (0.7cm) wire tail.

3 *Hammer the frame.* Use the hammer to flatten the wire frame. Hammer one side flat, then flip it over to hammer the other. After hammering, use round-nose pliers to make sure the loop is closed. Use a surface that can handle the impact of hammering, like a workbench or a bench block.

4 *Attach the gemstone.* Cut a 6" (16cm) length of 24-gauge wire. String the gemstone teardrop onto the wire and center it. Wrap one end of the wire around the bottom edge of the hammered frame, creating a coil. Repeat on the top side of the frame.

5 *Add the coils.* Cut a 30" (76cm) length of 24-gauge wire. Coil the wire snugly around the bottom of the loop at the top of the frame, and continue to coil the wire down around the teardrop bead and frame. At the desired length, trim the wire and tuck it underneath the coils.

6 *Add the earring wire.* Attach an earring wire to the loop at the top of the frame.

7 *Make the other earring.* Repeat Steps 1–6 for the matching earring.

SHOPPING LIST

• 2 - 16 x 9mm faceted gemstone teardrop beads
• 12" (31cm) - 16-gauge wire (gold)
• 72" (185cm) - 24-gauge wire (gold)
• 2 - Earring wires (gold)

TOOLS

• Needle-nose pliers
• Round-nose pliers
• Wire cutters
• Jewelry hammer

TECHNIQUES

• Forming a Loop
• Wrapping Beads with Wire

Tip: Don't hammer the wire too thin: the thinner you hammer the wire, the more likely it is to snap.

Crystal Pendant Necklace

With its sparkling crystal pendant and shiny beads, this necklace will bring a bit of bling to your wardrobe. Pair it with a t-shirt and jeans or dress up the ensemble with a sharp blazer or jacket.

Level:
♦ ♦ ◦

Time:
♦ ♦ ◦

1 *Start the necklace.* Cut two 23" (59cm) lengths of beading wire. Thread both lengths of wire through the holes of the druzy crystal pendant so that the pendant is positioned in the very middle of the beading wires.

2 *Add beads.* Starting on one side of the pendant, string 3 rondelle beads onto both beading wires.

3 *Add beads and the clasp.* Separate the two wires and bead about 8½" (22cm) of purple seed beads onto each wire. Bring the wires together and pass them through another rondelle bead. Using a single crimp tube on both wires together, connect the necklace to one half of the toggle clasp.

4 *Repeat.* Repeat Steps 2–3 on the other side of the necklace, attaching the other half of the toggle clasp to this side.

5 *Add the chain.* Cut an 18" (46cm) length of dark purple/gold chain. Using jump rings, connect one end of the chain to each half of the toggle clasp.

SHOPPING LIST

- 1 - 36 x 28mm druzy crystal pendant (white)
- 8 - 10mm rondelle beads (AB purple)
- 520+ - 11/0 seed beads (purple mix)
- 18" (46cm) - 2.3mm cable chain (dark purple/gold)
- 46" (120cm) - Beading wire (silver)
- 2 - Crimp tubes (silver)
- 2 - 4mm jump rings (silver)
- 1 - Large toggle clasp set (silver)

TOOLS

- Needle-nose pliers
- Crimping pliers
- Wire cutters

TECHNIQUES

- Opening and Closing Jump Rings
- Attaching Crimp Tubes/Beads
- Cutting Chain
- Forming a Loop

Desert Turquoise Necklace

Embrace the bold style of this necklace by pairing it with other desert-inspired colors like bright corals and oranges. If desired, make two extra teardrop bead drops in Step 6 and attach them to earring wires for a matching set of earrings.

1 *Cut the chain.* Cut one 2" (5cm) and three 6½" (16.5cm) lengths of chain.

2 *Create the bead links.* Slide a small melon bead, a medium melon bead, and a small melon bead onto an eye pin and form a loop to make a bead link. Repeat to make a total of 2 bead links.

3 *Create the extender chain.* Slide a small melon bead, a medium melon bead, and a small melon bead onto a 2" (5cm) head pin and form a loop to make a bead drop. Use a 4mm jump ring to connect this bead drop to one end of the 2" (5cm) chain to make a beaded extender chain.

4 *Create the necklace chain.* Use 4mm jump rings to join the following to make the necklace chain: 6½" (16.5cm) length of chain, bead link from Step 2, 6½" (16.5cm) length of chain, bead link from Step 2, and 6½" (16.5cm) length of chain.

5 *Add the clasp.* Use a 4mm jump ring to connect a lobster clasp to one end of the necklace chain. Use a 6mm jump ring to connect the beaded extender chain from Step 3 to the other end of the necklace chain.

6 *Create the teardrop bead drops.* Slide a small melon bead, a bead cap, a turquoise teardrop, and a filigree gold round bead onto a head pin and form a loop. Repeat to make a total of 8 teardrop bead drops.

7 *Create the faceted bead drops.* Slide a small melon bead, a filigree gold round bead, and a faceted gold round bead onto a head pin and form a loop. Repeat to make a total of 7 faceted bead drops.

8 *Add the central bead drop.* Use a 4mm jump ring to connect a faceted bead drop to the bottom of the middle link of the entire necklace chain.

9 *Add the rest of the bead drops.* Use 4mm jump rings to add evenly spaced alternating teardrop bead drops and faceted bead drops to either side of the central bead drop from Step 8. You should end with a teardrop bead drop just a few chain links before each bead link from Step 2.

SHOPPING LIST

- 8 - 26 x 13mm teardrops (turquoise)
- 7 - 9–10mm faceted abstract round beads (bronze)
- 8 - 10mm decorative bead caps (gold)
- 21 - 4 x 5mm melon beads (gold)
- 3 - 7 x 9mm melon beads (gold)
- 15 - 8mm filigree round beads (gold)
- 23" (59cm)   3mm curb chain (gold)
- 16 - 2" (5cm) head pins (gold)
- 2 - 1" (2.5cm) eye pins (gold)
- 21 - 4mm jump rings (gold)
- 1 - 6mm jump ring (gold)
- 1 - Lobster clasp (gold)

TOOLS

- Needle-nose pliers
- Round-nose pliers
- Wire cutters

TECHNIQUES

- Opening and Closing Jump Rings
- Cutting Chain
- Forming a Loop

Periwinkle Necklace

In shades of purple and blue, this necklace will look great with your favorite pair of jeans. Or dress it up as a statement piece—try it with a cream sheath dress. You can also substitute the blue and purple beads for more vibrant colors to suit your style.

1 *Create the small bead links.* Slide a beehive bead, a bicone, and a beehive bead onto an eye pin and form a loop. Repeat to create a total of 8 beehive/bicone bead links.

2 *Create the large bead links.* Slide a large dark blue gemstone bead onto an eye pin and form a loop. Repeat to make a total of 3 dark blue gemstone bead links. Slide a light blue gemstone bead onto an eye pin and form a loop. Repeat to make a total of 4 light blue gemstone bead links.

3 *Create the bead link chain.* Connect the beaded links from Steps 1–2 together in this order: a beehive/bicone bead link, light blue gemstone bead link, beehive/bicone bead link, dark blue gemstone bead link, beehive/bicone bead link, light blue gemstone bead link, beehive/bicone bead link, dark blue gemstone bead link, beehive/bicone bead link, light blue gemstone bead link, beehive/bicone bead link, dark blue gemstone bead link, beehive/bicone bead link, light blue gemstone bead link, and beehive/bicone bead link. Connect the last loop on each end of the bead link strand to a separate 6mm jump ring.

4 *Create the second bead chain.* Cut a 16" (41cm) length of beading wire. Use a crimp tube to connect one end of the wire to one of the 6mm jump rings from Step 3. String the following onto the wire: 3 bicones and 1 beehive bead. Repeat to string on a total of 13 sets of 4 beads, leaving off the final beehive bead to finish the strand. Use a crimp tube to connect the end of the wire to the other 6mm jump ring from Step 3, so that the entire new strand lies above the bead link strand from Step 3 when both pieces are laid flat on the table.

5 *Create the third bead chain.* Cut a 14" (36cm) length of beading wire. Use a crimp tube to connect one end of the wire to one of the 6mm jump rings from the previous step, so it lies above the other crimp tube connected to that jump ring (above the second bead chain from Step 4). String the following onto the wire: a beehive bead, bicone, beehive bead, rubber-coated bead, beehive bead, bicone, beehive bead, and a light blue glass bead. Repeat to string on a total of 5 sets of 8 beads, leaving off the final light blue glass bead to finish the strand. Use a crimp tube to connect the end of the wire to the other 6mm jump ring from Step 3, so that the entire strand lies above the other crimp tube connected to the jump ring (above the second bead chain from Step 4).

SHOPPING LIST

- 4 - Medium/large gemstone beads (light blue)
- 3 - Medium/large gemstone beads (dark blue)
- 5 - 8mm assorted rubber-coated beads (periwinkle)
- 4 - 8mm assorted glass beads (light blue)
- 58 - 6mm crystal bicone beads (AB purple/blue)
- 49 - 5mm beehive beads (silver)
- 30" (77cm) - Beading wire (silver)
- 10" (26cm) 3mm curb chain (silver)
- 4 - Crimp tubes (silver)
- 1 - 3" (7.5cm) extender chain (silver)
- 15 - 1" (2.5cm) eye pins (silver)
- 1 - 1" (2.5cm) head pin (silver)
- 3 - 6mm jump rings (silver)
- 1 - 4mm jump ring (silver)
- 1 - Lobster clasp (silver)

TOOLS

- Needle-nose pliers
- Round-nose pliers
- Crimping pliers
- Wire cutters

TECHNIQUES

- Opening and Closing Jump Rings
- Attaching Crimp Tubes/Beads
- Cutting Chain
- Forming a Loop

6   *Add the curb chain.* Cut two 4½" (11.5cm) lengths of curb chain. Attach one end of each length of chain to the 6mm jump rings that all the beaded strands are attached to.

7   *Create the bead drop.* Slide a bicone and a beehive bead onto an eye pin and form a loop to make a beaded drop. Attach this beaded drop to one end of the extender chain.

8   *Finish the necklace.* Use a 4mm jump ring to connect one end of the curb chain from Step 6 to a lobster clasp. Use a 6mm jump ring to connect one end of the other curb chain to one end of the extender chain from Step 7.

Beaded Wrap Bracelet

This design is just fun! It's a perfect summertime accessory to pair with shorts and flip-flops. Have fun selecting buttons in different shapes and colors to express your unique style. You can also switch up the color of the cord or the beads.

Level:
♦ ♦ •

Time:
♦ ♦ •

1 **Prepare the cord.** Cut a 70" (180cm) length of satin cord. String the button onto the cord and slide it to the center of the cord. Holding the two cord ends together, tie them in an overhand knot just below the button shank. Place the button underneath the clip on the clipboard so the loose cord ends hang down.

2 **Attach the monofilament.** Cut a 9' (275cm) length of monofilament. Using a surgeon's knot, tie one end of the monofilament onto the left satin cord, just below the knot under the button shank.

3 **Attach the first bead.** String a bicone onto the monofilament and position the bead between the two cords. Holding the bicone in place, thread the monofilament under the right cord, then around and over the right cord and back through the bicone. Next, thread the monofilament over, around, and under the left cord.

4 **Continue attaching beads.** String on another bicone and continue repeating Step 3 until the bracelet is long enough to be wrapped twice around the wrist, making sure each bead is snug up against the previous bead. Secure the loose end of the monofilament to one of the satin cords using a surgeon's knot. Trim away any excess monofilament.

5 **Form the loop closure.** Hold the two satin cord ends together and tie them in an overhand knot just beyond the last bicone. Then tie a second overhand knot with the cord ends, leaving a space between the two knots large enough to slide the button through.

6 **Finish the cord ends.** Tie an overhand knot on each cord about ¾" (2cm) beyond the last overhand knot from Step 5. Trim each cord end just beyond the final knot.

SHOPPING LIST

- 1 - Decorative button with shank
- 105+ - 4mm crystal bicone beads (AB clear)
- 70" (180cm) - 2mm satin cord (green)
- 9' (275cm) - 8 lb. monofilament (clear)

TOOLS

- Scissors
- Tape or clipboard

TECHNIQUES

- Overhand Knot
- Surgeon's Knot

Tip: The materials listed will make a bracelet to fit a 6½" (16.5cm) wrist. Adjust the number of beads and cord length for smaller or larger wrist sizes.

Eco Warrior Stone Necklace

This design has an earthy boho vibe that will look great with any casual outfit. Pair it with sandals that feature leather straps, fringe, or tassels.

1 **Attach the monofilament.** Connect four 4mm jump rings to the loop of an eye pin. Cut four 15" (38cm) lengths of monofilament, and use crimp tubes to connect a length of monofilament to each jump ring.

2 **Attach the clasp.** Thread the eye pin up through a copper cone and form a double loop. (Follow the instructions for forming a loop on page 15, but wrap the wire around the round-nose pliers twice.) Use a 6mm jump ring to connect the double loop on the eye pin to one half of the toggle clasp.

3 **String the beads.** String 4½" (11.5cm) of ecru E-beads, then 7" (17.5cm) of dark copper E-beads onto each length of monofilament.

4 **Connect the strands.** Using crimp tubes, connect a 4mm jump ring to each length of monofilament, just beyond the beads. Trim away any excess monofilament. Connect all four jump rings to one new 4mm jump ring. Connect that 4mm jump ring to the loop of an eye pin.

5 **Make the eye pin.** Slide the following onto the eye pin from Step 4: 1 copper cone (large end first), 1 dark copper E-bead, 2 ecru E-beads, 1 dark copper E-bead, and 1 copper cone (small end first). Form a loop at the end of the eye pin. Connect a 4mm jump ring to this loop. Set aside.

6 **Create the other side.** Repeat Steps 1–5 for the other side of the necklace.

7 **Attach the center section.** Cut a 12" (30.5cm) length of monofilament. Using a crimp tube, connect one end of the monofilament to the 4mm jump ring at the end of one of the necklace sides.

8 **String the center section.** String 7½" (19cm) of pink gemstone beads onto the monofilament from Step 7. Using a crimp tube, connect the free end of the monofilament to the 4mm jump ring at the end of the remaining necklace side.

SHOPPING LIST

- 14+ - Gemstone beads (pink hued)
- 300+ - 6/0 E-beads (ecru)
- 520+ - 6/0 E-beads (dark copper)
- 6 - 8.5 x 18mm cones (copper)
- 72" (185cm) - 8 lb. monofilament
- 18 - Crimp tubes (antique gold)
- 4 - 2" (5cm) eye pins (antique gold)
- 20 - 4mm jump rings (antique gold)
- 2 - 6mm jump rings (antique gold)
- 1 - Large toggle clasp set (copper)

TOOLS

- Needle-nose pliers
- Round-nose pliers
- Crimping pliers
- Wire cutters
- Scissors

TECHNIQUES

- Opening and Closing Jump Rings
- Attaching Crimp Tubes/Beads
- Forming a Loop

Tip: You can often use beading wire instead of monofilament for a project—they are very similar. Beading wire is especially useful if a project uses heavy beads.

Autumn Glow Necklace

The soft colors and delicate strands of this necklace make it a perfect piece to dress up or dress down. Pair it with flattering colors like a cream blouse and a green cardigan. Wear the cardigan to work, then leave it behind for a night out.

1 *String the first strand.* Cut a 26" (66cm) length of beading wire and string on the following: a bronze bicone and an aqua bicone. Repeat this pattern 53 more times until 108 beads have been strung (including the first 2). Finish with 1 more bronze bicone. Set the strand aside.

2 *String the second strand.* Repeat Step 1, but repeat the stringing pattern 57 times so 116 beads are strung (including the first 2). Finish with 1 more bronze bicone. Set the strand aside.

3 *String the third strand.* Cut a 26" (66cm) length of beading wire and string on the following: a bronze bicone, an aqua bicone, a bronze bicone, an orange/cream rondelle, a bronze bicone, an aqua bicone, a bronze bicone, and a green rondelle. Repeat this pattern 10 more times. Finish with the following: a bronze bicone, an aqua bicone, a bronze bicone, an orange/cream rondelle, a bronze bicone, an aqua bicone, and a bronze bicone. Set the strand aside.

4 *String the fourth strand.* Repeat Step 3, but repeat the stringing pattern 9 times. Finish with the following: a bronze bicone, an aqua bicone, a bronze bicone, an orange/cream rondelle, a bronze bicone, an aqua bicone, and a bronze bicone. Set the strand aside.

5 *String the fifth strand.* Cut a 26" (66cm) length of beading wire and string on the following: a bronze bicone, an aqua bicone, a bronze bicone, a lime green bead, a bronze bicone, an aqua bicone, a bronze bicone, a green rondelle, a bronze bicone, an aqua bicone, a bronze bicone, a lime green bead, a bronze bicone, an aqua bicone, a bronze bicone, and an orange/cream rondelle. Repeat this pattern 1 more time. Finish with the following: a bronze bicone, an aqua bicone, a bronze bicone, a lime green bead, a bronze bicone, an aqua bicone, a bronze bicone, a green rondelle, a bronze bicone, an aqua bicone, and a bronze bicone. Continue by repeating this entire step once in reverse. Set the strand aside.

6 *Connect the strands.* Using crimp tubes, connect the wire at one end of each of the five beaded strands to a single 4mm closed jump ring. Repeat with the wire at the other end of each strand and a second 4mm closed jump ring. Trim away any excess wire.

SHOPPING LIST

- 252 - 4mm glass bicone beads (bronze)
- 180 - 4mm glass bicone beads (AB aqua)
- 27 - 10mm glass rondelle beads (AB orange/cream)
- 27 - 10mm glass rondelle beads (AB green)
- 10 - 13mm acrylic oval beads (lime green)
- 2 - 8.5 x 18mm cones (copper)
- 12' (365cm) - Beading wire (gold)
- 14 - Crimp tubes (antique gold)
- 2 - 4mm closed jump rings (antique gold)
- 1 - 4mm jump ring (antique gold)
- 1 - 6mm jump ring (antique gold)
- 1 - Lobster clasp (antique gold)

TOOLS

- Needle-nose pliers
- Crimping pliers
- Wire cutters

TECHNIQUES

- Opening and Closing Jump Rings
- Attaching Crimp Tubes/Beads

7 *Attach the finishing strands.* Cut two 5" (12.5cm) lengths of beading wire. Using crimp tubes, connect one wire to each of the closed jump rings from Step 6.

8 *Finish the necklace.* Thread one of the wires attached in Step 7 through the large end and out the narrow end of a copper cone. Then string on a bronze bicone. Repeat with the remaining wire on the other end of the necklace.

9 *Attach the clasp.* Connect the remaining 4mm jump ring to the lobster clasp. Using a crimp tube, connect that 4mm jump ring to one end of the necklace. Using a crimp tube, connect the 6mm jump ring to the other end of the necklace.

Bronze Twirl Earrings

These earrings are big, bold, and fun with lots of playful movement and shimmer—perfect for a night out with the girls! Give your hair the same fun, playful look with a messy ponytail with lots of volume.

1 *Cut the chain.* Cut sixty-four ½" (1.3cm) lengths of chain.

2 *Make the bugle bead chains.* Slide a bugle bead onto a head pin and form a loop. Repeat to make a total of 32 bugle bead drops. Connect each bugle bead drop to the end of a ½" (1.3cm) chain to make 32 bugle bead chains.

3 *Make the mixed-bead chains.* Slide 2 bugle beads and one 6/0 E-bead onto a head pin and form a loop. Repeat to make a total of 16 mixed-bead drops. Connect each bead drop to the end of a ½" (1.3cm) chain to make 16 mixed-bead chains.

4 *Make the leaf chains.* Connect each leaf charm to the end of a ½" (1.3cm) chain. Repeat this step to make a total of 16 leaf chains.

5 *Shape the spiral.* Cut a 3-coil section of memory wire. Tug both ends of the wire to open up and elongate the coils in the wire to form a spiral about 3" (7.5cm) long. Form a loop at one end of the wire, attaching a leaf chain to that loop.

6 *Start stringing the chains.* String the following onto the memory wire: an 11/0 seed bead, a bugle bead chain, an 11/0 seed bead, a mixed-bead chain, an 11/0 seed bead, and a bugle bead chain.

7 *Finish stringing the chains.* Continue with the following: an 11/0 seed bead, a leaf chain, an 11/0 seed bead, a bugle bead chain, an 11/0 seed bead, a mixed-bead chain, an 11/0 seed bead, and a bugle bead chain. Repeat this pattern 14 more times. Then, finish with an 11/0 seed bead.

8 *Attach the earring wire.* Form a loop at the end of the memory wire, attaching an earring wire to that loop. Trim excess wire if necessary.

9 *Make the second earring.* Repeat Steps 1–8 for the matching earring, making sure the coil rotates in the opposite direction from the first earring.

SHOPPING LIST

- 32+ - 6/0 E-beads (purple/blue/bronze metallic mix)
- 128+ - 11/0 seed beads (purple/blue/bronze metallic mix)
- 128+ - Bugle beads (purple/blue/bronze metallic mix)
- 32 - Leaf charms with jump rings (copper)
- 6+ - Coils memory wire, 1½" (3.8cm) diameter
- 8' (245cm) - 2 x 3mm cable chain (copper)
- 96 - 1" (2.5cm) head pins (antique gold)
- 2 - Earring wires (antique gold)

TOOLS

- Needle-nose pliers
- Round-nose pliers
- Wire cutters
- Memory wire cutters

TECHNIQUES

- Opening and Closing Jump Rings
- Cutting Chain
- Forming a Loop

Beaded Stripes Necklace

This bold necklace will be the star of any outfit. Have fun creating the small bead links by playing with beads in different colors and sizes. If you prefer warm colors, try this design with gold findings and red and orange beads.

1   *Cut the chain.* Cut the following lengths of chain: one 7¼" (18.5cm), one 5" (12.7cm), and four 1¼" (3.2cm).

2   *Create the large bead links.* Slide the flat oval accent bead onto an eye pin and form a loop to make a bead link. Slide a white swirl trapezoid onto an eye pin and form a loop to make a bead link. Repeat to make a total of 2 trapezoid bead links. Slide a mirror round bead, aqua nugget, and mirror round bead onto an eye pin and form a loop. Repeat to make a total of 4 aqua nugget bead links.

3   *Create the center of the necklace.* Connect each end of the teal oval bead link to the middle links of the 5" (12.7cm) and 7¼" (18.5cm) lengths of chain. Continue by connecting each side of a white trapezoid bead link and two aqua nugget bead links to the chains on either side of the teal oval bead link. Space the bead links so that they fan out from the shorter chain to the longer chain on each side of the central bead link.

4   *Create the small bead links.* Create a variety of 50 bead links by sliding different colors and size combinations of seed and E-beads onto single eye pins and forming a loop. Make 2 matching sets of 25 bead links (50 bead links total) of the following sizes: sixteen 1¼" (3.2cm) bead links, three 1" (2.6cm) bead links, three ¾" (1.9cm) bead links, and three ½" (1.3cm) bead links.

5   *Connect the small bead links.* Use a 4mm jump ring to connect the top and bottom of a single 1¼" (3.2cm) bead link to one side of each length of the 5" (12.7cm) and 7¼" (18.5cm) chains. Continue by using 4mm jump rings to connect the remaining fifteen 1¼" (3.2cm) bead links, three 1" (2.6cm) bead links, three ¾" (1.9cm) bead links, and three ½" (1.3cm) bead links. In the end the bead links should match on each side. Add extra jump rings between bead links where needed so the bead links lay nicely; you may need to add 6 or more extra jump rings on each side.

SHOPPING LIST

- 1 - 25 x 40mm flat oval accent bead (teal)
- 2 - 30 x 24mm trapezoid beads (white swirl)
- 4 - 16 x 20mm glass faceted nugget beads (aqua)
- 250+ - 6/0 E-beads (turquoise/metallic green/dark green mix)
- 430+ - 11/0 seed beads (teal/turquoise/blue/green mix)
- 8 - 4mm round beads (mirror silver)
- 20" (51cm) - 3mm curb chain (silver)
- 57 - 2" (5cm) eye pins (silver)
- 120+ - 4mm jump rings (silver)
- 1 - 18mm toggle clasp set (silver)

TOOLS

- Needle-nose pliers
- Round-nose pliers
- Wire cutters

TECHNIQUES

- Opening and Closing Jump Rings
- Cutting Chain
- Forming a Loop

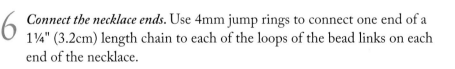

6 *Connect the necklace ends.* Use 4mm jump rings to connect one end of a 1¼" (3.2cm) length chain to each of the loops of the bead links on each end of the necklace.

7 *Add the clasp.* On one end of the necklace, use a 4mm jump ring to join the ends of the two chains together and connect them to one half of the toggle clasp. Repeat on the other side of the necklace with the other half of the toggle clasp.

Crisscross Cascade Set

Embrace your inner Jackie O and highlight the chic simplicity of this design with an outfit that features bold blocks of black and white. This set also makes a great go-to for a casual night out with the girls.

BRACELET

1 **Start the bracelet.** Slide a bugle bead onto an eye pin and form a loop to make a bead link. Use a 4mm jump ring to connect one end of the bead link to one half of a silver toggle clasp.

2 **Create the first link.** Slide a black bead and a bead cap onto a head pin. Thread the head pin through the second loop of the bugle bead link from Step 1. Then slide on a bugle bead and form a loop to make a bead drop.

3 **Create the second link.** Slide a black bead and a bead cap onto a head pin. Thread the head pin through the loop of the bead drop from the previous step and form a loop to make another bead drop.

4 **Repeat.** Repeat Step 3 twenty-one more times, referencing the photos to make sure the bead drops are facing in the right direction.

5 **Finish the bracelet.** Use a 4mm jump ring to connect the loop of the last bead drop to the other half of the toggle clasp.

EARRINGS

1 **Start the earring.** Slide a black bead, a bead cap, and a bugle bead onto a head pin and form a loop to make a bead drop.

2 **Create the second link.** Slide a black bead and a bead cap onto a head pin, and thread the head pin through the loop of the bead drop from Step 1. Slide on a bugle bead and form a loop to make another bead drop.

3 **Repeat.** Repeat Step 2 three more times, referencing the photos to make sure the bead drops are facing in the right direction.

4 **Finish the earring.** Connect the loop of the last bead drop to the bottom loop of an earring wire.

5 **Make the other earring.** Repeat Steps 1–4 for the matching earring.

SHOPPING LIST

- 33 - 8mm glass round beads (black)
- 33 - 4mm bead caps (silver)
- 34 - Lined bugle beads (silver)
- 33 - 1" (2.5cm) ball head pins (silver)
- 1 - 1" (2.5cm) eye pin (silver)
- 2 - 4mm jump rings (silver)
- 2 - Earring wires (silver)
- 1 - Toggle clasp set (silver)

TOOLS

- Needle-nose pliers
- Round-nose pliers
- Wire cutters

TECHNIQUES

- Opening and Closing Jump Rings
- Forming a Loop

GLOSSARY

Here are a few more miscellaneous terms you might encounter in the Shopping Lists in this book and in the jewelry aisles at your local craft store. For the definitions of most other tools and materials mentioned in this book, see pages 8–11.

Miscellaneous Terms

AB: standing for "aurora borealis," a type of bead finish applied to one side of the bead that reflects different iridescent colors.

druzy crystal: a stone with many tiny, fine crystals on top of a colorful mineral. They are very sparkly and colorful.

extender chain: a short length of chain used at the clasp to make the size of a jewelry piece flexible.

lariat: a necklace style that has a long, straight drop coming from the middle of the necklace. This type of necklace usually does not have a clasp.

Key Types of Chain

cable chain: chain that has interlocking links that are either round or oval in shape.

curb chain: chain that has interlocking links that are semi-curved and seem to interlock on an angle, allowing the chain to lie flat.

flat-link chain: any chain that has interlocking links where each link is somewhat flattened on its sides.

double-link chain: any chain that has two links paired up in place of single links.

drawn cable chain: cable chain with links that are stretched/elongated.

rope chain: chain that has multiple layers of links connected in a spiral-esque pattern, creating a rope effect.

figure-8 chain: chain that has figure-8 shaped links.

Features of Key Materials for Beads/Pendants

glass: very widely available, cheap to expensive, many different cuts and shapes.

crystal: widely available, cheap to expensive.

acrylic: widely available, affordable.

resin: less widely available, affordable.

gemstone: widely available, affordable to expensive, heavy weight.

INDEX

Note: Page numbers in *italics* indicate projects.